MW00878387

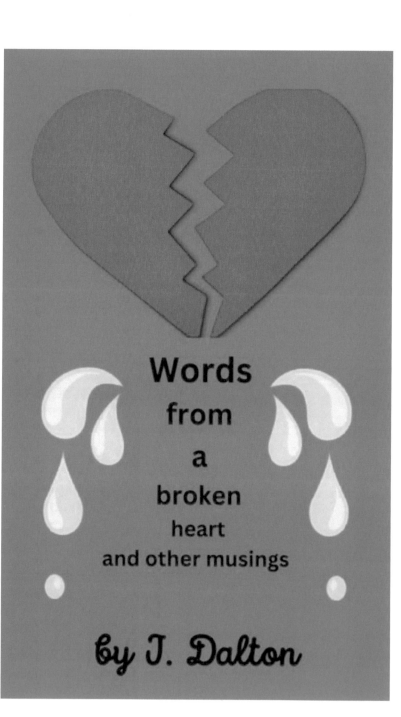

Words

from

a

broken

heart

and other musings

by J. Dalton

This book is dedicated
to my wife.
54 years together was not
enough!
I will find you,
and we will live another
half century in another time,
another place.

Don't cry for me when I'm gone.

I've lived a good life.

I've loved.

I've been loved.

We've helped the less fortunate.

We raised a family that I'm proud of.

What more do you want from life, other than more time?

Just know I will always love you

Betsy

Many of these poems are dark, and were written during the last months before my wife passed and shortly thereafter.

They were a way for me to express my feelings without putting an additional burden on my family.

I hope you enjoy them, but don't cry for my loss.

Cry with happiness for all the love we shared!

Table of Contents

Table of Contents

Really?

After all these years together, NOW you have
to leave me?

Really?

Through all the temptations, I kept my vows.

'cause I meant them.

Really!

You raised our kids, mostly by yourself,

And man, they turned out fine.

I was always off working, day and night,

following that dream of mine.

But now you have to leave me?

Really?

What about the plans we made?

The places we meant to go?

Veranda Beach,

Our little pool,

The fire pit out back?

So now you're gonna leave me?

Really?

How am I gonna live alone,

without you by my side?

More than a half-century together this time,

It's been one hell of a ride.

But now you had to leave me?

Really?

Even though you've left me, I'll love you for
all time.

You know we'll meet again,

Somewhere down the line.

We've done this thing before.

I'll see your face, and our hearts will know,

And things will be just fine.

No…

Really.

Cause I still love you!

Really!

There's a hole in my heart

There's a hole in my heart

Where you used to live

Once filled with love

That you'd freely give

Now you don't live there

You moved to my brain

Moving there hurt me

Caused me such pain

One thing I've learned

Don't trust your brain

Cause I always knew

You'll never leave

My brain or my heart.

That's where you've been

Right from the start.

Oh, darlin...

Oh, darlin…

It' almost midnight, and

I'm goin home now.

I've done everything I'm supposed to do here, so

I'm goin home now.

Tell the kids I love them,

I hope that they all knew.

I'm goin home now.

By the way, I love you too.

But I'm goin home now.

Gonna wait till you've all left the room, cause

I'm goin home now.

We all will be together

Someday soon, but

I'm goin home now.

Heaven's callin,

And it's gonna be soon, so

I'm goin home.

Don't cry for my leavin…

I'm goin home now.

Look what we made here,

Goin home.

I love you,

And I'll see you soon…

At our new home.

In Heaven.

When the day is nearly over

When the day is nearly over,

And night comes creeping in,

That's when it's the hardest

To hold the tears within.

Lying in bed without you

is the hardest thing I do.

That's because, my Love

This pillow's just not you.

The rain coming down

The rain's coming down

It's pounding the ground

Turning dormant plants

To green, from brown.

But what about me?

I need the Sun

The smile of a stranger

A baby's bubbly laugh

A hug from a friend

To kiss you again

That's what I need

To mark this winter's end.

As I walked through the woods today

As I walked through the woods today,

the canopy of trees

darkens the daylight…

and so too my mood.

Off in the distance,

shadows of something dark,

suspended in the branches

of trees long dead, shedding bark.

The closer I get,

The more I can see.

It's pieces of me.

Hanging,

strung up in a tree.

My soul has died

since you left me.

The Sun sinks below the horizon

The Sun sinks below the horizon

The world begins to turn dark

Just like my heart

Getting through the daylight

Without you gets easier

I just pretend you are still at work

But when the bustle of the day

Settles down

My smile turns upside down

Eating dinner all alone

No one to talk to

Re-runs on TV

The memories of you

worm their way

Into my heart

I push them away

So the tears don't start

But it never works

And sleep comes hard

I miss the us we used to be

And never will be again

My love for you will never end

I had a dream last night.

I had a dream last night.

I danced across Texas

with you in my arms.

How sweet to once again

Smell your sweet charms

Your favorite perfume,

Strawberry shampoo

Wafting up from your hair

It's hard to remember

That you are not there

That's the thing about dreams

You don't need to be here

not even near

You may be gone

but you live in my heart

and that my love

is all I need,

we'll never part

What do I do now

What do I do now

With the love we used to share?

I can't love the kids more

And you're no longer there.

I'd give that love to others

But billions of people, just aren't enough

To share all our love

Man, it's getting tough

To live this life alone

Our house just ain't the same

It may still our home

But the stone in the graveyard

Now bears your name

And without you here,

Nothing is the same.

How like me

How like me

Thought the old man

as he sat on his porch

lighting his pipe from the flame of the torch

That dried up old weed and I've

Outlived our usefulness

We're ready for the can

We've both spread our seed

now a future version can

Raise their young

to enjoy their time,

out here in the sun

for one day, they too

will be done.

Oh, what I wouldn't give

Oh, what I wouldn't give

To see your face,

To hear your voice,

To smell the scent of you

Once again.

How many times

have I turned to tell you something?

To share a laugh,

or just see your smile?

But, you're not there.

Little things remind me of you.

Little things remind me of you.

Things you used to say,

And things you used to do,

Things that our children

now do too.

And I smile,

Because in them

You still live.

People treat you different

People treat you differently

after your partner dies.

They move to avoid you,

won't look you in the eyes.

I'm still the same old person

There's just a hole

Now in my heart.

I'm trying to recover.

Please, just do your part.

As she took her last breath

As she took her last breath

A tear ran down her cheek.

Not for the loss of her life,

but for the new one she would seek.

She traveled across the stars

a ball of energy was she

looking for somewhere to land.

Someplace where she could be

But she'd already found it

That place...

Was inside me.

You are gone forever

You are gone forever

And I struggle

Every day

To find a way

To fill the void

you've left behind.

Time moves

More slowly now

And nothing will

be the same

And that, my love

Is what makes me

The saddest of all today.

I loved you enough to let you go

I loved you enough to let you go

To not be selfish, and so

You slipped into

the after life

Where soon we all must go

So that's where I'll find you

Once again, you know.

Silly Poems

Kevin was a Klepto

Kevin was a Klepto

A petty thief was he

All around him knew it

But clever, that was he

He played the simple fool

No suspect could he be

But when he pulled a diamond heist

He said,

"No, it can't be me.

I'll take your pencils

Your car keys too

But diamonds,

Never!

They're too rich for me."

It's all an illusion

It's all an illusion

all in your head.

You heard me,

believe what you've read.

The clouds are not moving

it's the Earth that's on a spin.

It happens over and over

again, and again.

She opened her laptop

She opened her laptop

on the desk by her bed

stories wandered around in her head

horrible demons all dressed in red

she wrote the story,

but she wanted them dead

Out on the sidewalk eyes glowed in the dark

something evil was lurking

right there in the park

Lock your door tonight

Lock it tight.

Things are moving around in the night.

Life seems different

Life seems different

looking down the barrel of a gun.

No place to turn, no place to run.

Seconds seem like hours.

Minutes pass like days.

Your very existence goes by in a haze.

Do what he asks

slow movements, for sure.

With a bullet to the head

there is no cure.

Water Lillies

Water Lillies

on the face of the pond

What lies beneath

used to be blond

Feet bound in cement

Didn't she know?

Rules are not to be bent

FAFO

Now no one one knows

Just where she went.

Things keep spinning

Things keep spinning

Round and round.

Like a record that's come to its end.

Oh, if only

I could reach out...

And speak to you

once again, my friend.

They tied themselves to the pier as a joke

They tied themselves to the pier as a joke,

then were surprised when the tide broke.

The water rose,

The knots, they swelled

louder and louder for help they yelled.

Water to their lips,

loudly they shout out.

Sorry, but...

Fuck around,

and find out.

Animal Poems

My little cat joins me

My little cat joins me

Each night up in my bed.

She sniffs my ear,

my eye, my nose

and sometimes all my head.

Does she really love me?

Or is she trying to decide?

What part of me to eat first

If she finds I'm not alive?

Tiger, tiger in the night

Tiger, tiger in the night

takes a swipe with his right

blood now spouts from his trainer's chest

one day later they put him to rest

A threat to humanity they all cried in fear

death to the killer far and near

Now they all go

to a video show

just to see the animals

that are no more

Giant Butterfly

Giant Butterfly

The child inched closer

a friend he might be.

Antennas are twitching

trying to see.

Friend or foe

What could it be?

All was good

at first, she thought

Until it attacked,

and alive,

she was not.

Karen loved to smell the flowers

Karen loved to smell the flowers

Lilacs, Cherry & Rose

She leaned in close

and took a big sniff

and got a big bee

right up her nose.

A horse is a horse

A horse is a horse

of course, of course

a beautiful steed is he.

A rider on back

holding his mane

whipping the steed with the reins.

Racing like lightning

faster he runs

across the western plains.

Oh look, he thinks to himself,

A tree with a low branch

sticking out like a shelf.

then turns and heads that way.

Ignoring the pain in his mouth.

Under the branch he runs.

Damn you, Silver!

He hears him yell

As he looks back with a smile

The rider picks himself up

He'll be walking for quite q while.

There's a mouse in the house

There's a mouse in the house,
The cats all a twitter!

There's a mouse in the house,
She thinks it's gonna get her.

There's a mouse in the house,
Don't know if I can sleep now.

There's a mouse in the house,
Catch it?
Kitty knows how.

There's a mouse in the house,
They're all around me,
Look out, I shout!

There's a mouse in the house,
My moneys on the cat.

There's a mouse in the house,
Would you look at that.

There's a mouse in the house,

It all just went so quiet.

There's a mouse in the house,
No longer a riot.

There was mouse in the house,

It's now a pile of cat puke!

Hunter/Killer

My hero!

Flying crocodile

Flying crocodile

Up in the sky

looking for dinner

from way up high

Keep track of Fifi

and your cat, Boo

Or they will be dinner

and you could be too.

Oh, how she wished she could stay out in the sun

Oh, how she wished she could stay out in the sun

Soaking up all the rays

If she could, she would

stay out on a rock

for days and days.

Too bad her flesh

was made of scales

That dried up in the sun.

Being a mermaid was great and all

but sometimes, like this

a look like a raisin

Was just not much fun.

Abstract poems

They called it the

They called it the

"Outhouse from hell"

Hot on a mid-summer's day

frost on the walls in winter

But she'd had chili for dinner,

and didn't want to go in.

The seat was made of tin

Ring around your bottom

No matter the season

She had to do it

No denying the reason.

Rock-a by-baby

Rock-a by-baby

in the tree top.

Why are you up there?

Make it all stop!

That's it, stop laughing!

This is no joke.

What if he falls

What if the branch broke?

Don't stand there and smile.

You're grounded forever,

Or at least for a while.

Maybe longer if you don't stop with that smile

I'm never again leaving

you two alone.

Kevin, just wait

Till your father gets home.

A secret message only lovers knew?

A secret message

only lovers knew?

Written in ink,

Black?

Or Blue?

The colors mattered

The slant did too

but each one meant

"I Love You!"

I stubbed my little toe.

I stubbed my little toe.

Don't want to let you know.

But it hurts me so.

That damned little toe

Tears fall down like rain.

I can't take the pain.

It hurts me so.

I think I must have

A case of toelio!

Politicians said

Politicians said

move Earth close to the Sun.

Scientists said

Oh, yes. It could be done.

Don't mess with Mother Nature

leave it the way it should be

Now, the Sun is oozing

from Earth's gravity

You think it's hot now?

Just wait till it's done.

You can't just travel at nighttime

to get closer to the Sun.

People say they're sorry

People say they're sorry

You've had bad luck, you know

But I just tell them

it's not bad luck and so,

Everything that happens

It's how our love can grow

My true love found me

Before I could go wrong

We shared a life together

A half century long

How can things be bad

With your lover by your side

Sure, there's ups and downs

But life's a special ride

There were times when I needed help

And times like that for you

But in the end, you loved me

And oh, did I love you.

As I walk through my version of hell

As I walk through my version of hell

my sinuses start to swell.

Pollen to the left,

Pollen to the right.

My eyes are so swollen

I've about lost my sight.

The flowers are so pretty

When they begin to bloom

But that's the time of year

That spells my nostril's doom.

The Table was set with white linen

The Table was set with white linen

The good dinnerware set out with care

For the 1st time in years

Soft candlelight lit the room.

Re-creating that old romantic night

He hoped she would remember

A flicker of a time long passed

If not, then the gesture

Would be new for her

He wanted to see her smile

Cause his love would always last.

Giant cherry tree

Giant cherry tree

Behind the house

Branches reaching skyward

Shading my old house

Struck by lightning

You took the shot

Memories for sure

We've got a lot

Home to nature's creatures

Their nests

You managed to hide

So many pictures

Taken through the years

Marking the growth

Of children, and you, of course

The time has come, you know

It's no longer safe below

Your trunk is rotten

You have to go

I'll really miss you

I hope you know

Seeing you gone

Will bring on more tears

Thank you for being

A friend through the years

Works

from my writing group prompts

The sign said "Come in and Visit!"

The sign said "Come in and Visit!", but that was really just a scam, for once you walked through the orange fluorescent door, you were transported to another place, another time, another world.

Plants that we had come to recognize as being a deep green color, were now different shades of orange and blue. The scents were stronger here. More fragrant and sweet, everywhere you went.

The plants were the same ones as we had back home, as well as all the insects and animals, but the different minerals in the air here were refracting the sunlight so that our eyes picked up the subtle differences in the pigments differently. Our minds wanted to see them the way we were used to seeing them, but it only took moments before the realization set in. This was what beauty was all about.

This was not Earth.

That was not our Sun.

We were in a different Galaxy.

We no longer lived in a world where we were black, white or brown. Out here, in this world we were all a beautiful purple color, and that changed the minds of so many that followed us through the door.

Kisses seemed sweeter.

A gentle touch, more soothing.

A smile from a stranger, was something that filled your heart.

No more hate, just love.

We now knew.

We were all just one race.

We were all the human race, and the fact that the door had been one way didn't matter to any of us anymore. When I asked someone what this place was called, they told me, "Why, it's Heaven, of course."

The pages of the open book turned slowly

The pages of the open book turned slowly in the orange scented breeze that drifted in from the open window, as if some shadow presences were reading the words.

"How could this be?" he thought to himself. "This was her favorite book, and it's been sitting closed, on her nightstand since the night she passed. "No one has been in her room since, so how did it get out here on the kitchen table?"

Things like this had been going on for the last several months and he asked the goldfish, "Is this a sign from beyond? She used to talk to you when she fed you, so do you know? Do you even have a clue?"

But all the fish did was mouth the word O, over and over, until he gave up and moved on.

As he bent to pick up the book, the words on the page seemed to shimmer, calling him, insisting he look. Without realizing why, he read the printed words of a Native American Shaman aloud.

Fear not my child, for life on Earth is but a moment in time, and death is the transition to an existence far greater than you can imagine. In time, you too will join us and know all there is to know in the universe. You will understand why we exist in several planes, and why we learn from so much pain. You will find love like you have never known and reconnect with those that have gone before.

Your soul is immortal and lives forever, reappearing as a solid being often so you can learn, and teach others lessons they need to know.

Sometimes it is joyous, sometimes it is painful, but you, the real you will never really die. Only the physical body you inhabit ceases to function.

Rejoice in this knowledge my child. We will meet again, and again, for time is just a figment of the imagination. Something that mankind made up to put order in his life. We slip back and forth in this existence and others and carry those memories with us. That is why certain souls are drawn to each other, over and over again.

So, do not weep for my passing, but have joy in the sharing of what we have had together, as we will meet again.

He closed the book and held it to his chest as a wave of calm swept through him.

He smiled as a butterfly landed on the flowers she had planted in the window box.

"Thank you, my love. I needed that."

They called her "Baby Blue

They called her "Baby Blue".

T'was a difficult birth,

right from the start.

Her mother struggled and pushed,

doing her part.

Two weeks late,

weighing ten pounds eight,

she came out all blue,

gasping for air.

Everything about her was blue, including her hair!

Her first word was "blue",

That's certainly true.

As she got older, that's when they knew.

There was no color other than blue,

that was all she knew.

The grass beneath her feet,

the color of the bed sheet.

The emotions she would feel

The flowers in the field

The color of the steel.

The songs the birds would sing,

came out like B. B. King.

Blues, baby. The blues.

But Baby Blue didn't care

She traveled here and there.

Love the life you get, she said

Cause it ain't over yet!

Her name was
Ester Scuttlebrick

Her name was Ester Scuttlebrick

But no one ever knew.

They only called her teacher

or, Mrs. Pink would do.

The schoolhouse door was painted pink

The wooden siding too.

The children, they all loved her.

Couldn't wait to get to school.

Each morning before class,

She fed the children cookies.

Sweet frosting colored pink

and strawberry flavored milk.

Served in a large tall glass

For the children to all drink.

The lessons, smooth as silk.

The children,

well behaved

And so polite to you.

The lessons, they'd repeat at night,

so the parents knew them too

The old pink schoolhouse

was the place to send your child

if they were sometimes wild

The towns folk, they all loved her

Until the day she died

Someone found her recipes

up high and in the back.

A place for her to hide

a leather keepsake,

locked and all in black.

The cookies and the milk you know

were the secret to her success.

"A drop or two of laudanum

Puts an unruly child at rest.

Increase the drops of laudanum

The older that they get.

No need to have commotion

In the classroom,

At least, not yet."

Like Rapunzel

Like Rapunzel, she was trapped inside this tower on another world, remembering a time back on old Earth when she could be outside with her friends, enjoying the sunshine, smelling the flowers or riding the giant Ferris wheel and going to the beach on the shores of the Atlantic Ocean.

Those days were gone now.

Now, she was alone on her father's island. Stuck here on a planet that held no hope for her escape.

The battles that had taken place in the skies above had filled the atmosphere with the atoms of spaceships and their occupants so that the sunlight was refracted through a haze that turned everything blue, including her mood.

It was only at night, when the twin moons finally rose over the horizon, that her mood would change. Then, she could see the other worlds out there. Distant places where life could exist. Where she could once again find love.

If only she could find a way off this planet.

What was wrong with all the beings throughout this galaxy? Why was everyone so intent on killing everyone else? There was enough room in the Universe for everyone to find a place to live, but there was always some other being that wanted what you had.

These stupid little stones.

That was what all this had been about.

Death and destruction for stones?

Let them have them, she had pleaded. They're just stones.

But the politicians said, "They're our stones, and no one is going to take them from us."

They meant nothing to us, but to the others…

They were worth killing and dying for.

Don't they know?

Love is the only thing worth fighting for.

Now, there is no one left on either side to love.

There is just me.

And I am alone.

In this tower.

Like Rapunzel.

The deeper he went

The deeper he went, the harder it became to breathe.

Not because he was winded

But because he sensed danger.

Down and down, he went

Thirteen levels.

Six thousand six hundred sixty-six steps.

He knew because he had counted every one.

He stopped at each level

and looked at the paintings on the doors there.

Where they led, he had no idea, but

The drawings became darker and darker in theme
the deeper he stepped.

There was evil here.

He could sense it.

Smell it.

Almost taste the bitterness of it.

The beautiful flowers that lined the steps near the
top

Morphed into dead barbed vines as he watched.

A blackness began creeping into his soul as he neared the bottom.

Stepping out onto the floor,

putrid sulfur smelling water began pouring in from all sides.

He reached out and called to those above for help,

But none was coming for the damned.

Somewhere, up above he heard a door slowly squeak open.

"Hello?" he cried, desperate for help.

"Is someone there? Dear God, I need help!

The water is rising! It's up to my chin, and I can't swim.

A deep chuckle echoed throughout the vastness of the chamber.

"You cry out for help from your God

but, where is he?" boomed the voice.

Has he thrown you a rope?

Has he walked on the water to grasp your hand?

Your God can not reach you here.

Only the unclean reside at these depths."

"Who are you? Show yourself. Help me, please."

"If I help you, you will owe me, will you not?"

"Yes, yes! Please, hurry.

The water is at my mouth now

and I'm standing on my toes.

I'll pay you anything you want."

"Anything?"

"Yes, anything. Just hurry."

"Then I want your soul," came the voice,

echoing with laughter throughout the chamber.

"What? you want my soul?

What kind of nut case are you, anyway."

"The kind that can save your pitiful life, Human.

"Who are you, really?

I am called many things.

Lucifer, yetzer hara, the Antichrist, Beelzebub,

Mephistopheles, the Prince of Darkness and others,

but you can call me Satan,"

he replied as he stepped out of the shadows and offered his hand.

Six months

Six months.

She pulled into the old dirt driveway, parked in front of the garage and listened to the tick, tick, tick of the engine as it cooled. His garage. His sanctuary.

There was no way she was going to even start to go in there today. That was just too much for her right now. Maybe tomorrow, or the next day. Maybe, the day after that if she could get up the courage.

It had taken six whole months to clean up all the legal junk after his death, but finally, yes finally, she was doing it. Cleaning out the old home. The garage would be the last place to clean.

She sat there for a moment, smoking the last of her cigarette and looking at the big dumpster sitting in the yard, and thought…

"So many memories are going to go the dump, never to be seen again."

Daddy had been such a cold man, she thought to herself. *"I can't remember the last time he hugged or kissed me or told me he loved me. Did he? Did he love me? At all?"*

She stubbed out the last of the smoke and flung the butt at the dumpster. She dug in her purse and found the set of keys the lawyer had given her. Then, taking a deep breath, stepped out and headed towards the house.

"Stale," she thought as she opened the door. *"A few open windows should help cure that,"* and set about fixing the situation, lighting a few of the scented candles her mother had scattered around the house.

"Now that that's taken care of," she thought, *"Where to start? The closet seems a likely place. I'll gather all of Daddy's old clothes and donate them to charity."*

She spent the next three hours stripping the hangers of her father's clothes and shoving them into plastic garbage bags. The smell of his Old Spice cologne still clung to his shirts and a few of his suits and, for an instant, she was back as young child on Sundays, sitting in row six on the left side of the church, between momma and him. They all had their heads down in prayer, but she was looking at the tattoo of an anchor on daddy's ankle, where his pant leg had risen just enough for her to see. Instantly, she was in the front row at mommy's funeral, standing next to him as he struggled to sing Amazing Grace while wiping the tears from his face.

Shaking her head and returning to the now, she saw the stack of boxes, stuck back in the corner and covered with a sheet. She pulled off the cover, and after sneezing from breathing in the dust, she opened the first one and there, sitting on top of a stack of pictures, was a little red camera. With shaking hands, she picked up the box and moved to the bed. Setting the camera to the side, she pulled out the first photo.

It was from the last time they had been together. Her mother's memorial. All their friends had gathered together and set the red lanterns free. A message of love and hope for another connection, another lifetime together. *"When had he taken that picture?"* she thought to herself. *"She didn't remember him with the little red camera, ever."*

Hours passed, and darkness crept through the window before she came upon the pictures of her. Each one had the date, place and time carefully inscribed on the back, written in his bold script.

"Little Ellen, 2/14/1952. My Valentines baby. I couldn't be more proud."

"Little Ellen, 6/29/1957. Graduation from kindergarten. Proud daddy!"

On and on they went. Every event, every birthday, nearly every moment.

Then, she saw the picture from their vacation in London. They had been strolling along the River Thames, where her mother complained about the smell of dead fish wafting up from below. She had spotted the red telephone booth, and running ahead, stepped inside, closed the door and started taking off her clothes like superman.

"Look, up in the sky. It's a bird. It's a plane. No, it's Super Ellen!" Those words came back to her now as if

he had just spoken them. *"Where did he hide that camera all those times? How had she not known? How could she have doubted his love all these years?"*

Now, she knew. He had been raised in a different time, a different world where it just wasn't proper for a man to show his love or his affection, and she sat there on his bed and cried.

Not for him.

Not for her.

But for everything they had missed.

It was an old fence

It was an old fence, scabbed up with whatever could be found around the old estate. Scraps of plywood, rusting metal sheets and old pallets, all fastened together in a hodgepodge arrangement that looked like a mad man had designed it.

The gate was homemade and several layers of chipping and peeling paint had been covered over with a coat of a disturbing pink that had probably come from a mixture of leftover cans.

The rusted old hinges cried out in protest as the gate swung out, allowing the inquisitive young intruder access to the grounds.

Inside, the former grandeur of a time long gone, struggled to maintain the status quo as once well-tended rose gardens poked their perfumed buds up through the weeds, seeking the spring sun and warmth. The dichotomy of the one-time beauty of the gardens and the ugliness of the fence surrounding the building was not lost on the young man.

The mansion didn't interest him... yet. For now, the huge storage building was what he was headed for. Who knows what the crazy old man that used to live here, has secreted away in there, he thought to himself. Maybe, there was an old car or motorcycle still in there. Maybe something even more exotic, like a plane or speedboat.

The young man walked around the outside of the building, looking for a way in, hoping there weren't guard dogs hiding somewhere, waiting to attack an unsuspecting intruder. Seeing none, he picked up a rock and used it break the glass on a back window. Reaching inside, he unlocked it and swung it aside, then climbed in.

Empty! The building was empty except for a single bowl of steaming soup, sitting smack dab in the middle of the floor. This didn't make any sense. No sense at all.

As he approached it, he could see a small note. There, spelled out neatly in flower petals words that simply read, "Eat me".

He couldn't help himself and picked up the bowl, brought it to his lips and took a sip.

Delicious! Warm, sweet like sugar, and a delightful aroma of fresh cut flowers. Lifting the bowl, he drank it all.

The room began to spin, and as he finally saw what was really inside the building, he gasped.

It was an old-fashioned gaming arcade. Thousands of units, stacked to the roof, complete with flashing lights and signs, all beckoning him to play. Off in the corner, dozens of skeletons large and small were stacked against the wall.

The screens played the same message, over and over…

Welcome to Grandpa's Video Arcade, where thousands of games can be played. Choose wisely my friend, or your life it will end. One game, no more. For only a win will open the door.

Good luck.

"I wonder"

"I wonder", she thought as she looked up at the sky, "what life would be like on a faraway world. Would it look like ours? If you could travel those far distances in a ship, what would they look like as you got closer? Would they all be shaped like a ball, like they say ours is, or would some of them have funny shapes like flat, or square, a triangle or maybe just pieces of dirt floating in the air.

I hope they look like home. Our home. Round and beautiful. Wouldn't it be fun if they were all different colors? Imagine a world that was a blue orb, or white or purple. Would there be people there? Would they look like us? And what about the plants? I would love to see plants that weren't all purple like they are here on our world. Can you imagine a green colored plant, or maybe even pink?

If there are people living on other worlds, do they live their lives like we do? Do they have nice things like bathrooms and plenty of food, or do they struggle just to find a way to live?

Daddy says I ask too many questions, but if you don't ask, how do you get answers?

When I go to sleep at night, I sometimes dream I can travel to other worlds in a blink of an eye. I don't know how that happens, but then I see other places. People too. Not exactly like us, but close. Some have different colored skin and hair on different parts of their bodies. Some are dirty and they fight over stupid things like owning land, or food. Some, live in a fantastical world where they lack for nothing. Their only desires are to gain more knowledge and help others. I like that dream.

Daddy says I should stop smoking this funny cactus I found in the desert, but the people living there say it has magic powers stored inside. Plus, I like the way it makes me feel.

The sky is beautiful tonight. I think I'll just lie here a bit more and see where I end up.

She raced down
the stairs

She raced down the stairs of the tenement, her flowered dress fluttering behind her as she took the steps two or three at a time.

Breathless, she checked the battered mailbox looking for the letter she hoped he had sent.

Tossing the bills aside, there it was.

The letter. His letter. To her.

She let out the breath she didn't realize she had been holding, and with shaking fingers, tore the envelope open.

"My dearest Ellen," it read, and her heart soared. "My dearest. He lead off with my dearest. That's me!" she smiled to herself.

My dearest Ellen,

It is with a broken heart that I must tell you that I am leaving you. It's not that I don't love you, I do. The last few months have been heaven with you. It's just, well, this is very difficult for me to tell you, but… I am already married. My wife and I had a big fight last year and she threw me out. She wants me to come back and try to rebuild our life for our kids.

I know. We talked about getting married and starting a family of our own, but my kids need me, and I have to try to fix this for them.

I've left you the blue bomber out front. Unfortunately, it has a flat left front tire. I left you some cash under the cushion of the sofa to get it fixed.

I'm so sorry about this, and I am ashamed I never told you about it.

Don't try to find me. I've taken a cab across the bridge to San Francisco and will be living under my real name.

I wish you all the luck finding someone new.

Love,

Andrew

"You son of a Bitch!" she screamed as she crumpled the letter into a tiny ball and threw it out into the street. "Is that even your real first name you liar? What do expect me to do? Go back to my own husband? He's probably got someone new by now."

She finally understood the saying, Karma's a bitch.

The air seemed to shimmer

The air seemed to shimmer as she stood outside the door to her old house.

How long had it been since she had been back? Thirty, forty years? Probably it was closer to fifty, now that he thought about it.

Funny, but it still looked the same from the outside.

The storm door had the same old dent right smack in the middle where Billy hit that foul ball playing in the front yard back in the early 60's. He's been gone now, going on ten years.

Time passes, but memories just fade a bit, she thought.

Reaching out, her hand seemed to pass through some sort of wave, surrounding the house. She knocked on the door.

No one answered, but there were definitely noises coming from inside. Was the door unlocked? She turned the handle and the door swung wide, still making that squeaking noise it had so many years ago.

"Ethel," cried out a deep male voice that sounded a lot like her father.

"Bring me in some of that al-u-min-i-um foil, will ya? This damn TV lost its signal again. I need to upgrade the damn rabbit ears."

That sounded exactly like daddy. She remembered him saying those very words dozens of times.

"One second, Harold," came the woman's voice from the kitchen."

Ethel, Harold? Those were her parent's names. What were the odds of the new owners having the same names of her mother and father. She stepped deeper into the front hallway and looked into the living room. There, sitting in his recliner, was her father! A man who had been dead for almost forty years. And, sitting on the floor by his feet, was a younger version of herself, looking at a stack of pictures.

What was going on here? How could this be happening. She was fifty-six, and yet, there she sat as an eight-year-old girl.

"Momma? Daddy? Can you hear me? Can you see me?" she cried out. No answer came from either of them.

"Daddy! Please listen to me. Do not. I repeat, do not go out to the store on Christmas Eve of 1988. There will be a man there that robs the store, and you get shot and die trying to save the lady that runs the place. Please Daddy. Listen to me! Don't go.

But of course, no one heard Eileen. She was just a ghost, visiting her past, in a place called, The Twilight Zone.

Karen regretted

Karen regretted using superglue to fix her glasses. It would be days before she could use her right hand to do anything other than look stunning holding the frames.

Going up and down the stairs now presented an interesting problem as she couldn't grab the railing unless she was against the left side.

Her brother Kevin had warned her, and now she would have to live with the shame. A shame that brought tears, every time she poked herself in the eye with the frame. Why did it have to be her little brother that said that word? "Duh!" How could one three letter word hurt so deeply?

Even walking in the gardens had created problems. With her allergies, how could she blow her nose when those damned glasses were stuck to her hand? Going to the bathroom? She didn't want to think about that.

In order to avoid questions when meeting others, she would stop and strike a pose, asking "Aren't these glasses stunning?" Then, she would take them off and use them to emphasize her words.

Never again, she thought.

Never again.

Like Archimedes

Like Archimedes supposedly did when he tried to defend the city of Syracuse in 213 B.C., Nico took his mirror out to cliffs at the edge of the ocean. He focused on reflecting the sunlight on the incoming wooden fishing boats that were slipping through the calm blue waters off the shores of Greece, intending on setting them on fire.

Nico was not a normal boy.

Nico hated anything that wasn't blue or anything that disturbed the stillness of that hue. That's why his parents painted their home his favorite shade of blue.

Ignoring the tear in the butt of his old blue jeans, he bent over the edge of the cliff to see if the ships were now in flames.

The people screamed in horror as the edge of the cliff gave way, and Nico and his mirror plummeted down to the rocks below.

Every year since then, the townspeople have made a memorial to Nico in the days leading up to the anniversary of his tragic death. A pair of blue sneakers, like the pair he was wearing that day, are set out at the top of the cliff. One by one all the young unwed girls place a single daisy inside them.

Some say, on stormy nights at the bottom of the cliffs, you can still hear Nico scream.

They sat in silence

They sat in silence, with only the occasional noise of a page being turned in a book breaking the stillness of the morning.

"I'm bored. Let's all go out and have a cup of tea at that new shop right next to Hardie's gin mill, and we can talk about all the people we don't like," said Beth as she closed the book she was reading.

"That sounds like fun," agreed the rest of the small book club. After putting their writing materials away, they headed out for an afternoon of fun.

Four hours and three pots of tea passed and the owner finally let them know it was five P.M and time for him to close.

"I'm having so much fun with you girls. Let's not go home yet. What do you all say to going next door and have a mint julip or two before we call it a night?" said the youngest member, Jane. "All in favor, raise their hands."

"Does raising two hands count for anyone that doesn't want to go?" asked Bridgette.

"It doesn't matter. It's a unanimous decision anyway," came Beth's infectious laugh. "Forward march troops. Straight ahead to the parlor of alcohol."

The girls pushed the swinging doors aside and stood there with their hands on their hips and the setting sun at their backs like they were old west lawmen, looking for a robber.

"Barkeep!" shouted Jane. "Drinks for me and my friends, and put it on my tab." Then, she burst out laughing as they made their way to a table and piled their things in the booth beside it.

Six hours later, the bartender decided they had had more than enough alcohol to kill any infectious disease they might be carrying, so he shut them off and called two Ubers for them so they wouldn't get caught driving drunk and cause him to lose his license.

On the ride home, Beth was not feeling well and asked the driver to pull over as she thought she might get sick.

"Roll down the window and stick your head outside," he said as he looked for a place to pull over. "You puke in my cab, and you pay for the clean-up.

Unfortunately for Beth, her head was too far out the window and too close to the power pole as the driver pulled over.

The moral of the story is, don't lose your head trying to have a good time.

She swore to him

She swore to him she had lived several lives before and was determined to convince him of that fact.

As she sat down at the old typewriter, she closed her eyes and let her fingers remember the old familiar muscle memories she had built up in one of the more recent lives. Here, in this time she was a data input specialist for the early years at NASA.

The memories of past lives came easy now. Suddenly, she was a man in this lifetime. A paratrooper with the 82 Airborne and he/she remembered flying over the fields of England on his way to Normandy and looking down out of the jump door.

Strangely, he had no fear at that point, trusting God would do his will, and with a slight push from the jumpmaster, he was falling towards the earth and the hell that was about to be foisted on the inhabitants below.

She could still feel the pain where the first bullet pierced his/her shoulder. Funny how things like that carried through time and different existences, but there it was. The Doctors could never find anything wrong, but she knew. It had happened on D Day, in another lifetime, and now showed as a small star of a birthmark.

They had been blown off course and had been late to arrive. The jump was supposed to be before dawn but was an hour overdue. That meant they didn't have the cover of darkness to hide in, and they became easy targets for the enemy sharp shooters. Just three of the squad survived the jump.

The farmhouse, ah yes. The window, nearly hidden behind the growth of the shrubberies, but inside? The family inside was so brave. They had taken him in and bandaged his wound, then hid him in the cold storage room under the barn.

She remembered these things now, like they hadn't happened 80 years ago to someone else. Clickity clack, clickity clack went the typewriter as she put the memories down on the paper. She closed her eyes and wept, remembering all the friends that had been lost that day. Young boys, really. Some who had never known the love of a woman other than their mother.

When she opened her eyes, she was no longer in Normandy in 1944, but on another world. In another time. In another body. A beautiful valley, bathed in the warmth of the morning sun.

In this time, peace ruled this world. Love, respect, sympathy. No humans inhabited this planet in this time, and that, she knew, was good.

The crunching of
the gravel

The crunching of the gravel driveway beneath the tires brought her home, faster than the airplane she had just recently departed.

Pulling up to the house, she noticed how the flowers in the garden still bloomed, even as the days were getting shorter, and the nights colder.

Winter was coming soon, and the darkness of the northern section of Canada would soon be upon them, much like the darkness that had fallen over their small family.

He had been a good dad. Steadfast and loyal to his wife, loving and kind to a fault with his kids. He tried to keep things up, but ninety-two years of hard work had taken its toll on him. Like the minister said, "God needed another good soul in heaven, and your father's name was on the top of the list."

As she walked up onto the old covered porch, she looked in the side window, just to get a peek before she opened the door.

Everything was exactly as she remembered it before she had gone off to teach. Everything that is, except the dust and cobwebs.

Opening the door, she brushed the web and the spider that had built it aside, then stepped in the house. No, she thought. This isn't just a house, this is home. This is where I grew up. Where I laughed and cried. Wept at my mother's death, right there on the couch. I couldn't stay here back then, and he couldn't leave. Funny how death affects different people differently.

She stood there and took it all in. All the books she had written were still on the shelves, but her father had turned the spines to the back, telling her he couldn't stand to look at them any more now that she chose to leave.

Well, she thought. Maybe he couldn't stand to look at them, but he couldn't throw them out, either. Love is complicated like that.

The old typewriter was still in the same old place, and it still had the same piece of paper her mother had been typing on before she died. It was yellowed and dusty now, but as she read it, she felt the sorrow all mothers feel as they give up some of their happiness for their children's.

Odd. The old clock on the table next to papa's chair had stopped at 1:21. The same as the time of death on his death certificate. Was it co-incidence, or a sign from the old man?

So many questions she wished she could ask, but now would go unanswered.

The old crone had said

The old crone had said, "Follow the arrow, child. It will take you where you want to go."

And so, he walked down this hallway that seemed to go on forever. Yet, no matter how many steps he took, he was always in the same spot. Room 1313. Twenty steps later, room 1313. Another twenty steps, another room 1313.

Was that where the woman said he was supposed to go?

Twenty steps more and yet another room 1313.

This time, he tried the handle, discovering it was unlocked.

Carefully pushing the door aside, he stepped into the room.

It was the smell he noticed first.

Sweet. As if someone had just placed a fresh cut bouquet of flowers in the room, but there was nothing here but a single peacock feather, stuck in a vase.

Stepping closer, he leaned in to see if that was where the smell was coming from and the eye of the feather blinked.

Startled, he backed away, but a voice spoke, not out loud, but as if a whisper inside his head.

Recognizing the voice of the old crone, she said… "You have found the key my child. Lick the eye of the feather and it will take you where you want to go."

Confused, but curious, he stepped forward and plucked the feather from the vase and brought it to his mouth. "Should I?" he thought. "Why not," and he stuck his tongue out and touched the eye of the feather.

Instantly he was moving. Round and round he went down a swirling blue hole that had opened beneath his feet.

He opened his mouth to scream but no sound came out as he plunged farther and farther down into the swirling vortex. He closed his eyes and prayed to his God to save him from this hell. Then, it all went black.

When he finally opened his eyes, there it was. The place he had always dreamed of.

He was on top of a cliff overlooking a beautiful bay on a warm summer day. The tropical breeze cooled him as the mist from the crashing waves rose up from the shore to settle on his skin.

But when he tried to move his feet, he found he was stuck in place and cried out…

"What's going on, why can't I move? I want to go down to the shore."

The old woman's voice came to him once again, saying… "That was not included in what you wanted child. Next time, be careful what you wish for.

The harvest is done

The harvest is done,

It's time to relax.

A bit of honey and rum.

An hour or two in the hammock

Should do

To cool this farm hand's soul.

You're up from dawn to dusk each day

when you work the land you love.

Now, a quick shower and then,

A short night

out on the town.

Celebrations don't come often out here

where the weather can get quite severe.

You take what you can, and do it again

Too soon it will be,

up at dawn

To feed the livestock again.

The moon slips out from behind the clouds

The moon slips out from behind the clouds

On a dark and stormy night.

A witch's brew,

And devils too

Prepare to give you a fright.

Keep your windows shut tight

Your doors locked too.

The vampire can't bite you

He can't come in

Unless you invite him to.

So don't let him in

It would be a sin

If he bit your neck too.

The creature from the black lagoon

Is waiting in the swamp.

Tonight, just stay inside.

Let kiddies have their romp,

but stay away from the swamp.

Or they'll be dinner too.

Once upon a time

Once upon a time,

In a land so far away

There lived a girl

Who played violin

All the night and day.

No one listened as she played her tunes

That made her sad

And she got mad

I'll show you what I can do!

She added a microphone

A wah-wah pedal

And amplifier too

Now she plays old rock songs

In front of growing crowds

While dressed in black

She takes them back

To the time of rock and roll

Where all the leaves are brown

And the sky is grey

On a soulful San Francisco day

Then, she kicks it up a notch

Or two or maybe three

An A/C D/C wanna-be

That's the girl for me!

The days are getting shorter

The days are getting shorter

Nights are cooling down

We need a fire now

To all gather round.

The bees have done their yearly job

Turning pollen into honey

That helps flowers grow

I think that's kind of funny

Children captured fireflies

And put them in a jar

I see the light now

Nature's such a show.

The flowers that the bees grew

Adorn a daughter's braid

She knows it's past their bedtime

And so,

She's not afraid.

They sat there for hours

This last work was originally written as three separate pieces.

The first section was written after my wife passed away, and I joined a writing group, just to force myself to get out of the house.

It was based on the writing prompt from picture #3 above, and reminded me of right after when my wife and I we came home from her being diagnosed with incurable small cell lung cancer that had spread to her bones.

We sat out on our deck, looking out over the woods behind our house and just talked about our lives together and how we/I would go on from here.

The middle section was written on one of the worst nights of my life. The insurance company would no longer cover my wife's hospital stay, and I couldn't find a nursing home or home care nurse to help out, so my son and daughter took turns helping me take care of my wife and one of us slept on the floor next to her bed, as she kept trying to get out of bed to go to the bathroom, but didn't have the strength to stand.

I was getting maybe three hours of sleep a night, and felt helpless. I didn't want to share that with my kids and put more stress on them, so I started writing down my feelings and then throwing the page away.

This page somehow got left in the tablet, and I found it after she passed.

The last section was written after I came home after she passed away at the end-of-life facility I finally found.

It took three months before I could read this aloud to anyone.

They sat there for hours. Just holding hands and staring out over the woods. The age-old language of love being conveyed not in the spoken word, but in the occasional gentle squeeze of the hand and a tear-filled smile.

How could he deal with the news?

She was his everything. The love of his life. She was his soul mate.

They had had plans. Big plans.

Plans to raise a family. Plans to build a home together. Plans to travel… see the world.

They were going to love life, live long, and grow old together.

But her diagnosis had changed all that.

They needed to live for the now.

But now… now wouldn't last for long.

His love for her…

that would last forever.

But that was three months ago.

Tonight?

Well… tonight he sat in his chair, in front of the fireplace at 2:50 in the morning and put his face in his hands.

Tears filled his eyes but he couldn't let them fall.

He couldn't let her see him crumble and lose hope.

He had to stay strong.

Keep smiling, telling her he loved her.

For her.

At least for a little while longer.

He wiped away the tears and thought to himself,

Love is a strange beast.

It can bring you unbelievable joy, like the birth of your child, or

it can bring you unbelievable pain as you watch someone you love suffer.

It's a living breathing beast all its own.

Filling your heart to overflowing at the first hint of love, then, draining your soul at the end.

You pour everything you have into those that you love, even to the point where you feel guilty for the 3-4 hours of sleep you try to get every night as you watch them waste away.

I need to be there for her now.

More than ever, I need to ease her pain.

But I no longer can.

I see her body wasting away and somehow, I feel guilty for not doing more.

I know it's a fight we cannot win, but her pain can't be worse than mine, can it?

Hers is dulled by the drugs.

Mine will never be.

She is the love of my life.

She is my wife, and I am helpless.

I close my eyes, but sleep evades my mind.

I'm searching.

Desperately searching for a plan B,

But there isn't one.

A gentle breeze stirs the curtains of the open window and her soul softly exits the room.

Somehow, the scent of her perfume fills his senses as he remembers.

All her troubles are left behind like discarded clothes as she is lifted up, no longer tied to her earthly body.

She is no longer in pain.

Floating above them, she sees him place one last kiss on her tortured body.

A single tear rolls down his cheek.

She is at peace now.

He will be too. Soon, but not now.

He knows he will find her again, but in this lifetime, there is a hole in his soul that can never be filled.

"I love you," he says, and brushes a strand of hair away from her brow.

"I always will."

"I love you too!" she thinks as she rises up.

And his heart is full again.

About the Author

I hope you enjoyed this little book.

Here is a little bit about me, and my main writing interest,

Science Fiction.

Except for work, I had never written anything in my life other than a note on a Christmas card or a sympathy card to someone whose family member had died. It never crossed my mind to be an author.

I had been feeling tired and basically run-down for several months, and even my co-workers had asked if I was alright. Like any man, I ignored all of the warning signs.

Then, in August of 2016, I had to go in for my yearly physical (required for the company's insurance policy), and of course, the Doctor had a blood draw done. The next day, the Dr.'s office called and wanted me to come back in and have another blood test done. The Dr. was concerned that there was a possibility that the previous test had been processed incorrectly. I went back, had the blood drawn, and the next day, the Dr. called and wanted me to go see a specialist. She thought I might have Leukemia because my white blood cell count was off the chart. The next day, (who gets an appointment with an oncologist in one day? That spooked me!) I had a bone marrow biopsy and was diagnosed with CML Leukemia (Chronic Myelocytic Leukemia). My world had just turned upside down! I stopped back into work and told my boss about it and that I needed to take the sick time I had built up, in order to fight this.

Over the next few weeks as I got sick from the high dose of chemo pills, I did a lot of thinking about what my legacy to my children and grandchildren would be. I didn't want them to just remember me from pictures and stories told while drinking at holidays, so I decided to write a story for them that they could have, and re-read to their children, and their children's children, and tell them about the crazy old man that started all of this silliness.

So, at the ripe old age of 64, I stepped off the edge of sanity, and wrote my first book, *"The Gates to the Galaxies!"*, & discovered that I actually like telling stories.

I'm a newbie to writing & really didn't know how to do research on historical things and, quite frankly, I didn't want to take the time I wasn't sure I had.

Writing Sci-fi allowed me to create a setting that existed in my mind. I could create an entire world, species, concepts that existed not in fact, but inside my head. It also allowed me to change the things that I thought were wrong with conventional sci-fi stories, like the over use of "Warp speed". In my book, they use folded space technology to travel through a galaxy and a "Gate" to go from one galaxy to another. I introduce several other unconventional concepts in each of the books in the series.

I always liked the thought of "what else is out there", but the original "Star Trek" got me hooked, despite the corniness and limited production qualities. It was just fun for a young kid with a questioning mind. The later versions became too politically preachy for me to really get into them.

The story arc throughout the series is always about good triumphing over evil. There are many different species that live and work together always for the good of each other. Looking back, I think that as I was writing, and especially in the second book, "*A Return to the Gates*" where I introduce a new adversary, (the 'Ones' and the Master and his twin brother the Successor), subconsciously I was thinking, good was going to conquer evil. (Leukemia).

I want people to open their minds to possibilities. Not just about space and time, but about the world around us. Just because it hasn't been done yet, doesn't mean that it's impossible.

I hope you enjoyed reading this book as much as I enjoyed writing it.

If you did, I would love it if you would go to my Amazon author's page,

https://www.amazon.com/J-Dalton/e/B08NF7NB3P/ref=dp_byline_cont_pop_ebooks_1

and leave a review.

Thanks again, and may you

"Live long and prosper."

Made in the USA
Columbia, SC
24 October 2024

44304156R00087